The Ten Positive Commandments

The Ten Positive Commandments

Susan L. Wilson

Contents

Honor Father and Mother

Kill Others with Kindness

Honor and Respect Spouse and Others

Bless God and Others with Giving

Build Others Up with Your Words

You are Jones, the King's Kid

Conclusions

Study Guide

Dedication

To all believers who have a heart for God

Chapter One

Introduction

Exodus 17 says that after a three month journey the Israelites are setting-up camp in front of Mount Sinai, where God wants to make a covenant with them. The covenant offers many benefits but also obligates them to obey God. The people agree to meet with the Lord God. Moses prepares the Israelites for the day they will meet God.

On the designated day, God descends on Mount Sinai accompanied by thunder, lightning and a terrible earthquake. Moses makes sure that the people understand they cannot go directly up on the mountain. Only Moses is allowed to go directly up the mountain. The stage is set, which was to shape the Israelites into a holy nation. God's chosen people are to be an example to all nations and they are to reflect God's character.

God gives the Ten Commandments. He gives the critical list which is the bases of spiritual and moral law. These principles were to provide guidance for all harmonies relationships with God and with one's fellow man.

There is quaking and smoke on Mount Sinai. God speaks to Israel from heaven. He is no fictitious God that someone made up. He is a real God that set up rules so people can have a better life. He tries to convey these rules to his people.

After God speaks to his people, the Israelites go to Moses and tell Moses that they want Moses to speak to God because they are afraid of Him.

Instead of falling on their knees and worshiping God, the Israelites rejected God by asking Moses to be a go-between. God sees what the people are doing. God is deeply hurt by these actions. Whether we want to believe it or not, God does have feelings. All He wanted to do is have a relationship with His people, the Israelites.

It says in Jeremiah 31:33 (all Bible verses are taken from the New King James Version (NKJ)), "But this is the covenant that I will make with the house of Israel after those days, says the Lord: I will put My law in their minds, and write it on their hearts; and I will be their God, and they shall be my people."

That is what God wanted for the Israelites. He wanted a relationship with them. God wanted to love and care for the Israelites.

God ended up having Moses going up to Mount Sinai and then giving him the law on stone tablets. The law ended up having many don'ts in it. The law has been seen in a negative light in which we have to obey them all or we go to hell. Instead of seeing the law as a negative bunch of rules and regulations that we have to live by, let's see them in a positive light. We need to see them as guidelines to help us get closer to God and our fellow man. When we fall, we can go to the Father and our fellow man and ask them to forgive us. We can go on with our lives. In this way we can proceed in having a wonderful relationship with God and our fellow man.

Having Christ in the mix, we now have open access to God to be able to talk to God and walk with God. We can even sit in His lap and give Him a big hug when things go wrong or right.

This is what God wants for us. This has been His plan from the beginning—to have a personal relationship with Him.

I will show you how we can use the Ten Commandments in a positive way and how we can build a closer relationship with God; Father, Son and Holy Spirit.

In Deuteronomy 6:4-6 we find, "Hear, O Israel. The Lord our God, the Lord is one.

"You shall love the Lord your God with all your heart, with all your soul and with all your might.

"And these words which I command you today shall be in your mind. And these words which I command you today shall be in your heart; you shall teach them diligently to your children, and shall talk of them when you sit in your house, when you walk by the way, when you lie down, and when you rise up.

"You shall bind them as a sign on your hand, and they shall be as frontlets between your eyes.

"You shall write them on the doorposts of your house and on your gates."

And Jesus adds to this, "Love your neighbor as yourself." This is how God wants us to start in our relations with Him.

Chapter Two

Worship God Only

The first positive commandment is to worship God and Him alone. Jesus said in his words to the woman at the well in John 4:21-24, "Woman, believe Me, the hour is coming when you will neither on this mountain, nor in Jerusalem, worship the Father.

"You worship what you do not know; we know what we worship, for salvation is of the Jews.

"But the hour is coming, and now is, when the true worshipers will worship the Father in spirit and truth; for the Father is seeking such to worship Him.

"God is Spirit, and those who worship Him must worship in spirit and truth."

This is the starting point. We need to realize that we don't need a special place to worship God. We can worship Him anytime and anyplace we want. Wherever we go and whatever we do, God is there with us.

In Isaiah 46:9-10 we find, "Remember the former things of old, for I am God and there is no other; I am God, and there is none like Me. Declaring the end from the beginning, and from ancient times things that are not yet done, saying, 'My counsel shall stand, and I will do all My pleasure.'"

Isaiah 45:5-7 says, "I am the Lord, and there is no other; there is no God besides Me. I will gird you, though you have not known Me, that they may know from the rising of the sun to its setting that there is none besides Me. I am the Lord, and there is no other. I form the light and create darkness, I make peace and create calamity; I, the Lord, do all these things."

Psalm 18:32 says, "It is God who arms me with strength, and makes my way perfect."

In these verses, we see God as the only God there is; there are no others. He is the one who created us. He is the one who protects us. He is the one who shows us the way through our dreams and visions. He is the one who gives us ideas on how to do things. He makes our way perfect. He is the Alpha and Omega, the beginning and the end, and He is the one who desires our praise, adoration and thanksgiving. He is the only one who can help you out of your messes.

God is the one who is for us. In Romans 8:27-32 we find, "Now He who searches the hearts knows what the mind of the

Spirit is, because He makes intercession for the saints according to the will of God.

"And we know that all things work together for good to those who love God, to those who are the called according to His purpose.

"For whom He foreknew, He also predestined to be conformed to the image of His Son, that He might be the firstborn among many brethren.

"Moreover whom He predestined, these He also called; whom He called, these He also justified; and whom He justified, these He also glorified.

"What then shall we say to these things? If God is for us, who can be against us?

"He who did not spare His own Son, but delivered Him up for us all, how shall He not with Him also freely give us all things?"

God is a good God. He gave us Jesus to take the penalty for our sins. He cared that much for us. That is how much he loves us. This is another good reason to worship God and Him alone.

Romans 8:35 states: "Who shall separate us from the love of Christ? Shall tribulation, or distress, or persecution, or famine, or nakedness, or peril, or sword?

"As it is written: 'For Your sake we are killed all day long. We are accounted as sheep for the slaughter.'

"Yet in all these things we are more than conquerors through Him who loved us.

"For I am persuaded that neither death nor life, nor angels nor principalities nor powers, nor things present nor things to come, nor height nor depth, nor any other created thing, shall be able to separate us from the love of God which is in Christ Jesus our Lord."

This encourages us to know that God is for us. He wants to hang out with us. He wants a personal relationship. He has done everything He can to help us be on His side.

The only one who keeps us from His love is ourselves. We are the ones who rejected Him through our worship of other things, such as money and ourselves.

In conclusion, this is an important commandment. God wants the best for us. By praising Him we bring His prescience into our lives. He starts making things work out for good rather than evil. He starts solving problems and showing us the way to go. In the end, if we listen and obey Him, He will say to each and every one of us (Matthew 15:23), "Well done, good and faithful servant. You have been faithful over a few things. I will make you a ruler over many things. Enter into the joy of your Lord."

Chapter 3

Honor God

The second commandment is honor God. This means God comes first in your life. What does that mean? When you wake up in the morning, you read your Bible. You take your journal out and listen to what God has to say to you. You have a written dialogue with God. You are probably asking yourself, how can I talk to God? Here is how you can talk to God.

First, you close your eyes and picture yourself in a special place with God or Jesus. You could be walking with Him along the Sea of Galilee. It could be in the dining room while having hot or cold drinks with God. God or Jesus and you could be sitting on the banks of the River of Life under the Tree of Life.

Second, have a pen and paper or journal available to write down the dialogue you have with Him. If you don't hear anything, ask Him a question. Write down the first thing that comes to your mind. You are probably asking yourself, how do I know it is from God or Jesus? If it is negative, it is from Satan. If it is positive, it is from God. Try doing this on a daily basis. It will help you to honor God.

Another thing you can do to honor God is to hold devotions at meal time. It helps your children to learn more about God. If that doesn't work, try to find family time to get together to do the devotions.

Third, you can honor God by talking to God throughout the day. Try talking to Him like you would talk to your friends. After all, God is one of your best friends that you could ever have. God knows everything you think and do anyway. So why not ask Him for suggestions on how you can improve on yourself. He will do things in a way that doesn't make you feel bad about yourself. God doesn't condemn people. He gently directs you in the right way. He also loves to hear from you. So try to communicate with God and he will answer you back. Be yourself.

One of the last things to honor God is to serve Him and your fellow man. In the parable of the sheep and the goats, He tells you what he wants you to do. Matthew 25:35-40 states: "'For I was hungry and you gave Me food; I was thirsty and you gave Me drink; I was a stranger and you took Me in. I was naked and you clothed Me; I was sick and you came to visit Me; I was in prison and you came to Me.' Then the righteous will answer him, saying, 'Lord, when did we see You hungry and feed You, or thirsty and give You drink? And when did we see You a stranger and take You in or naked and clothe You? Or when did we see You sick, or in prison, and come to You?' And the King will answer and say to them, 'Assuredly, I say unto you, inasmuch as you did it to one of the least of these My brethren, you did it to Me.'" So find out what you need to help others out.

As for myself, I have worked with disabled children. I have tried to make them feel like they are valuable people. I have encouraged my own disabled child, G. J., to do different things others have never tried before. His accomplishments were many before he passed away. He was a great artist. He drew pictures which will be put on Christmas cards. He wrote a song and it was published. He was an accomplished chef and served many good meals to others who needed them.

It is important to honor God. Ben Franklin one time was asked, "Why should we honor God? How do you know he even exists?" Ben Franklin replied, "God is alive. If you dishonor Him, He will judge you. If He judges you, you will know He exists. This will tell you He is alive and well."

Chapter 4

Praise God

The third commandment deals with praising God instead of swearing and taking the Lord's name in vain.

The first way to praise God is to bless God. Here are some ways to do it. Psalm 34:1 states: "I will bless the Lord at all times. His praise shall continually be in my mouth." Psalm 104:1 goes, "Bless the Lord, O my soul! O Lord my God, You are very great: You are clothed with honor and majesty." In Psalm 144:1 we find, "Blessed be the Lord my Rock, Who trains my hands for war, and my fingers for battle." As you can see, many positive things come to you when you bless the Lord. Your day seems to go better and you can feel his prescience.

The second way is by saying who God is. Here are some examples. Psalm 8:1 states: "O Lord, our Lord, how excellent is Your name in all the earth, You who set Your glory above the heavens!" In Psalm 18:1-2 we find, "I will love You, O Lord, my strength. The Lord is my rock and my fortress and my deliverer;

my God, my strength, in whom I will trust; my shield and the horn of my salvation, my stronghold."

Psalm 23:1 starts out, "The Lord is my shepherd. I shall not want." Psalm 27:1 states: "The Lord is my light and my salvation; whom shall I fear? The Lord is the strength of my life; of whom shall I be afraid?" Then Psalm 28:1 continues, "To You I will cry, O Lord my Rock: do not be silent to me, lest, if You are silent to me, I become like those who go down to the pit."

Psalm 46:1 reads, "God is our refuge and strength, a very present help in trouble." Psalm 93:1 continues, "The Lord reigns, He is clothed with majesty; the Lord is clothed, He has girded Himself with strength. Surely the world is established, so that it cannot be moved."

Exodus 3:14 says, "And God said to Moses, 'I AM WHO I AM.'" Genesis 17:1 states, "When Abram was ninety-nine years old, the Lord appeared to Abram and said to him, 'I am Almighty God; walk before Me and be blameless.'"

These verses show you who the Lord is and what He does, and helps you to know why He is worthy of praise.

The third way is to petition God for the answers to our problems. Here are some examples. Psalm 16:1 states, "Preserve me, O God, for in You I put my trust.

"O my soul, you have said to the Lord 'You are my Lord, my goodness is nothing apart from You.'"

Psalm 20:1 continues the theme, "May the Lord answer you in the day of trouble; may the name of the God of Jacob defend you." And Psalm 22:1 states, "My God, my God, why have You forsaken me? Why are You so far from helping me, and from the words of my groaning?"

Psalm 28 reads, "To You I will cry, O Lord my Rock: do not be silent to me, lest, if You are silent to me, I become like those who go down to the pit." Psalm 59:1 continues, "Deliver me from my enemies, O my God; defend me from those who rise-up against me." Psalm 51:10 states, "Create in me a clean heart O God, and renew a steadfast spirit within me." In Psalm 35:1 we find, "Plead my cause, O Lord, with those who strive with me; fight against those who fight against me."

God hears you. Sometimes God waits a while before He gives you an answer. Eventually God answers the question. You need to be still and listen to the answer. It may be the answer you want. It may not be the answer you want. Praising Him will help you see His answer clearly.

The fourth way to praise and thank God is through song. This puts you in a positive frame of mind. Here are some examples. Psalm 149:1 goes, "Praise the Lord! Sing to the Lord a new song, and His praise in the congregation of saints."

Continuing, we find in Psalm 101:1, "I will sing of mercy and justice; to You, O Lord, I will sing praises. Psalm 138:1 states, "I will praise You with my whole heart; before the gods I will sing praises to You."

In conclusion, the four ways to praise the Lord are to bless Him, say who He is, petition Him for answers, and sing to Him. All of these bring God's prescience to you. If you keep a journal, it will help you in many ways. You can get the help you want in your time of need. So why swear and use His name in vain? When you do this, you lose a close friend who can help you out.

Chapter 5

Hear God's Voice and Enter His Rest

The fourth commandment is hearing God's Voice and entering His Rest. What does that mean? To hear God's voice, we need to be quiet. We need to pick a day, time and place to physically rest from our labors. In Exodus 20:8-11 we find, "Remember the Sabbath day, to keep it holy. Six days you shall labor and do your work, but the seventh day is the Sabbath of the Lord your God. In it you shall do no work: you, nor your son, nor you daughter, nor your manservant, nor your maid servant, nor your cattle, nor your stranger who is within your gates. For in six days of the Lord made the heavens and the earth, the sea, and all that is in them, and rested the seventh day. Therefore the Lord blessed the Sabbath day and hallowed it." This gives us guidelines on what to do.

There are other things you can do need to do to hear God's voice and enter into His rest. The second way to hear God's voice and enter His rest is for you to get eight or more hours of sleep each night. It would be a good idea to take one day of complete rest. In this way God can speak to you in your dreams and impart to you a strategy on what to do with your life.

God can also heal your body. It is a good idea to record your dreams and visions in a notebook. In this way you can remember what He has said to you. If you don't understand a dream, ask Him to give you the interpretation.

The third way to her God's voice and enter His rest is to close your eyes and picture yourself with God or Jesus in a room, by the Sea of Galilee or River of Life. Then start asking Him questions. If the answers are positive, you know it is from God. If they are negative, you know they are from the enemy. Keep doing this on a daily basis. It is important to hear from God.

The fourth way to hear God's voice and enter His rest is to read God's word as contained in the Bible. Read God's word on a daily basis. It will speak to you. Write down what you hear. Share it with others. In this way you will get direction on the road you should take in your life.

The fifth way to hear God's voice and enter His rest is to fast from negativity. In Isaiah 58:6-12 we find, "Is this not the fast that I have chosen: to loose the bonds of wickedness, to undo the heavy burdens, to let the oppressed go free, and that you break every yoke? Is it not 'to share your bread with the hungry, and that you bring to your house the poor who are cast out; when you see the naked, that you cover him, and not hide yourself from your own flesh?' Then your light shall break forth like the morning, your healing shall spring forth speedily, and your righteousness shall go before you; the glory of the Lord shall be your rear guard. Then you shall call, and the Lord will answer; you shall cry, and He will say, 'Here I am.'" As you can see from these verses, when you do the positive things, God will hear you and respond to you.

The last and final way to keep the Sabbath holy is to worship together in church. In Hebrews 10:24-25 it says, "And let us consider one another in order to stir up love and good works, not forsaking the assembling of ourselves together, as is the manner of some, but exhorting one another, and so much the more as you see the day approaching." We need to assemble so we can hear the word of God and make sure we are hearing the word right. It is good to get each other's opinion of what the Lord is saying to us. We need accountability partners to keep us straight. The church does that. It keeps us from going into error.

These are the ways we can keep the Sabbath holy. Try to follow them on a daily basis and see how you can grow in the Lord.

Chapter 6

Honor Your Father and Mother

The fifth positive commandment is to honor your father and mother. Why should we honor our parents? The reason we need to honor our parents is because it is the first commandment that gives you a promise of a long and better life. It also promises you that things will go well for you on this earth. In Ephesians 6:1-3 we find, "Children, obey your parents in the Lord, for this is right. 'Honor you father and mother,' which is the first commandment with promise: 'that it may be well with you and you may live long on the earth.'"

Your earthly father helps you relate to your heavenly father. If you can get your relationship with your earthly father right then you can relate to your heavenly father. It is through our fathers that we get our identity; therefore it is very important for fathers to play and instruct their children. It is also important for fathers to listen to their children. In Ephesians 6:4 it states, "And you, fathers, do not provoke your children to wrath, but bring them up in the training and admonition of the Lord."

An example of this is in my own family. Growing up, my dad Harold always played games with us and taught us to listen to him for our own protection. He did it in a fun and loving way. That helped me see God as a dad who loved to be with me and play with me, but at the same time I learned to listen to God. Not all of you have a father that fits this model. As a father try to be that kind of father so that your children may know now to relate properly to our heavenly father, who is God.

Your earthly mother helps you to relate to the Holy Spirit. You are probably wondering how we can relate to the Holy Spirit through our mother. The best way to understand who the Holy Spirit is to go to John 16:7, which says, "Nevertheless I tell you the truth. It is to your advantage that I go away; or if I do not go away, the Helper will not come to you; but if I depart, I will send Him to you." In John 15:26 we find, "But when the Helper comes, whom I shall send to you from the Father, the Spirit of truth who proceeds from the Father, He will testify of Me." John 14:26 adds, "But the Helper, the Holy Spirit, whom the Father will send in My name. He will teach you all things and bring to your remembrance all things that I said to you."

The Holy Spirit is referred to as the Helper, or in other versions of the Bible, as the Comforter. If we look at Genesis 2:18-23 we find, "And the Lord God said, 'It is not good that man should be alone; I will make Him a helper comparable to him.'

"Out of the ground the Lord God formed every beast of the field and every bird of the air, and brought them to Adam to see what he would call them. And whatever Adam called each living creature, that was its name.

"So Adam gave names to all cattle, to the birds of the air, and to every beast of the field. But for Adam there was not found a helper comparable to him.

"And the Lord God caused a deep sleep to fall on Adam, and he slept; and He took one of his ribs, and closed up the flesh in its place.

"Then the rib which the Lord God had taken from man He made into a woman, and He brought her to man.

"And Adam said: 'This is now bone of my bones and flesh of my flesh; she shall be called woman, because she was taken out of man.'"

Women were considered a helper or a help mate to man. They were to complete the man and steer him on the right road. That is what the Holy Spirit does; it steers you on the right road. It is very important that women know the right path because they are the ones who will care for the children and direct them in the right way to go. Women are to support their husbands and are to build them up. They are also the go-between between the husband and the children. If a child does wrong the mother can talk with the child and find out what happened. Then she tells her husband what the situation was and smoothes things out. She is the backbone of the family. Without her the family falls apart. This is the same way the Holy Spirit works. The Holy Spirit corrects the God's children and smoothes things over with their heavenly Father.

God has shown me how we can put into practice the command to honor our earthly parents and our heavenly parents. We can dance on their ceilings. How can we do this? Every time we take a gift that our parents and others have mentored us with, we are dancing on their ceilings. An example of this is how Gary's love of mathematics has been displayed in our daughters' and granddaughter's lives. They are taking my husband Gary's gift of mathematics and using it in their careers or schooling. They are enjoying a gift he has given them. Gary may not realize it, but they are dancing on his ceiling. We all need to do that to honor our heavenly parents and our earthly parents. We need to take those gifts that are in us and dance on their ceilings.

Here are some proverbs about why honoring our parents is important.

1. "A wise son makes a glad father, but a foolish son is the grief of his mother." See Proverbs 10:1. You should make

your parents glad instead of putting sorrow and worry on them.

2. "A wise son heeds his father's instruction, but a scoffer does not listen to rebuke." See Proverbs 13:1. It is good to listen to your parents so you don't get into trouble.

3. "He who spares his rod hates his son, but he who loves him disciplines him promptly." See Proverbs 13:24. If you discipline your children it shows you care about them. If you don't discipline them it shows you don't care about them.

4. "Train up a child in the way he should go, and when he is old he will not depart from it." See Proverbs 22:6. If parents will raise their children in the right way, those children will give you honor.

5. "The rod and reproof give wisdom, but a child left to himself brings shame to his mother." See Proverbs 29:15. If a child is not disciplined and goes his own way, he will disgrace his mother.

6. "Correct your son, and he will give you rest; yes, he will give delight to your soul." See Proverbs 29: 17. Anytime you correct your children in the right way, you will be proud of them now and in the future.

In conclusion, I have shown you the way to honor your father and mother. I have also given you many reasons why you should honor your father and mother. To help you remember that you get your identity from your father and your nurturing from your mother. Starting with this commandment we switch from our relationship with God to our relationship with others. The next chapters will all deal with our relationship with one another.

Chapter 7

Kill Others with Kindness

The sixth positive commandment is to kill others with kindness. Why kill anyone with kindness? Perhaps they did horrible things to you. First, we need to define where murder comes from. In Matthew 15:19 we find, "For out of the heart proceeds evil thoughts, murders, adulteries, fornications, thefts, false witness, blasphemies." So murder is the one of the things that the heart produces. We find it in our hearts.

Second, murder can come as a result of anger. In Matthew 5:21-26 we find, "You have heard it was said to those of old, 'You shall not murder,' and whoever murders shall be in danger of the judgment.

"But I say to you that whoever is angry with his brother without a cause shall be in danger of the judgment. And whoever says to his brother, 'Raca!' shall be in danger of the council. But whoever says, 'You fool!' shall be in danger of hell fire.

"Therefore if you bring your gift to the altar, and there remember that your brother has something against you, leave your gift there before the altar and go your way. First be reconciled to you brother, and then come and offer your gift.

"Agree with your adversary quickly, while you are on the way with him, lest your adversary deliver you to the judge, the judge hand you to the officer, and you be thrown into prison.

"Assuredly, I say to you, you will by no means get out of there till you have paid the last penny." It doesn't pay to be angry with your brother over anything.

Third, murder comes from works of the flesh. In Galatians 5: 19-22 it states, "Now the works of the flesh are evident, which are: adultery, fornication, uncleanness, licentiousness, idolatry, sorcery, hatred, contentions, jealousies, outbursts of wrath, selfish ambitions, dissentions, heresies, envy, murders, drunkenness, revelries, and the like; of which I tell you beforehand, just as I also told you in time past, that those who practice such things will not inherit the kingdom of God."

The last thing that murder comes from is hatred. It states in 1 John 3:15, "Whoever hates his brother is a murderer, and you know that no murderer has eternal life abiding in him." Try not to go that route. You put yourself in hell.

How do we get rid of these things? The first thing we need to do is to recognize who we hate deep down inside. We usually hate those who we precede as our enemies. In Matthew 5:43-48 Jesus says, "You have heard that it was said, 'You shall love your neighbor and hate your enemy.'

"But I say to you, love your enemies, bless those who curse you, do good to those who hate you, and pray for those who spitefully use you and persecute you, that you may be sons of you Father in heaven; for He makes His sun rise on the evil and on the good, and sends rain on the just and on the unjust.

"For if you love those who love you, what reward have you? Do not even the tax collectors do the same?

"And if you greet your brethren only, what do you do more than others? Do not even the tax collectors do so?

"Therefore you shall be perfect, just as your Father in heaven is perfect."

How can I be perfect like God and really forgive my enemies? In Psalm 51:10-13 it says, "Create in me a clean heart, O God, and renew a steadfast spirit within me. Do not cast me away from Your presence, and do not take Your Holy Spirit from me.

"Restore to me the joy of Your salvation, and uphold me with Your generous Spirit.

"Then I will teach transgressors Your ways. And sinners shall be converted to You." Only God can help you clean up your heart and renew your mind. Spend time with God in his word and write down what He says. This will help you clean up your problems with others.

This will lead to forgiveness for the people you would like to murder. Many times they work out of fear. They are afraid you are a threat to them. They fear you will take their positions, or gifts and talents, away from them. After you forgive them, reconcile with them. If they will not reconcile, kill them with kindness.

In Matthew 5:38-42 it states, "You have heard that it was said, 'An eye for an eye and a tooth for a tooth.' But I tell you not to resist an evil person. But whoever slaps you on your right cheek, turn the other to him also.

"If anyone wants to sue you and take away your tunic, let him have your cloak also.

"And whoever compels you to go one mile, go with him two.

"Give to him who asks you, and from him who wants to borrow from you do not turn away."

By killing him with kindness he may change and become a friend. When you are in need, he will help you back. We need to show others the Jesus in us. This will help turn others to find Christ.

In conclusion, we need to make sure our hearts are clean. We need to ask God to clean them and restore a right spirit in us. We need to forgive everyone, even if they have done wrong to us. Then we need to reconcile with our neighbor. If a person does not reconcile with, us we need to kill him with kindness, until he comes to the point that God leads him into reconciliation.

A person starts seeing the Jesus in us when we follow Christ's commands. The name of God's game is to lead all people to Christ. At times it is a hard game to play. We have to realize it is not some person that is the enemy; it is Satin and his demonic angels that are the enemy. We have to see others that are in his camp as victims. Our mission is to help set them free from their prison.

Chapter 8

Honor and Respect Your Spouse and Others

The seventh commandment is to honor and respect your spouse and others. What does it mean to honor and respect your spouse and others? When you marry someone you take vows. The vows go like this: you should love, honor and cherish your spouse in sickness and health, for richer and poorer, until death do you part. Let no man put you asunder. This is done in most weddings but only a few people take it seriously. This vow means what the vow says.

When you marry a person there are going to be good times, but there are also going to be bad times. During the bad times, you need to remember the vows you have taken. You are not going to always live happily ever after. Your mate will fail you. You need to build him up, not tear him down. You need to be strong in the Lord and pick him up. It is important during these bad times to encourage and build a person back up. This is not easy. When my husband fell into pieces and lost control of his host personality, I had to find help and build him back up. It is not an easy thing to do. I had to rely on the Lord to look at the positive things he still had to build him up. After he had lost his job, I also had to find activities for him to do. He could no longer work. I had to go back to work and find jobs that could get us through these hard times. I had to sell the big house to supplement our income. At the same time we got a lawyer to help Gary to get his pension and social security. University Baptist Church was great spiritual, psychological and physical help to us in our time of need. Too many people dump their mates when a problem arises. This is a time when a person that is having problems needs to step up to the plate and seek help for that person. You need to be able to learn and take over their job if they are disabled or ill. You must prepare yourself for hard times.

How can I, or anyone else for that matter, be prepared for hard times? In marriage, how do I know what is the right thing to do? You need to look to the word of God, the Bible, for answers. Here are some scriptures that will help you.

1. Genesis 2:24, "Therefore shall a man leave his father and mother and be joined to his wife, and they shall become one flesh." What is the definition of wife? Webster's Dictionary says it is a married woman. It did not say married person. We need to know the truth about God's

word. We need to know that God created Adam and Eve not Adam and Steve. The whole Old Testament deals with who you can marry and who you cannot marry.

2. Leviticus 18:22-23, "You shall not lie with a male as with a woman. It is an abomination. Nor shall you mate with any beast, to defile yourself with it. Nor shall any woman stand before a beast to mate with it. It is perversion." See what the Bible says about abominable and preserve behavior? God's word is trying to help you live a happy and healthy life.

3. Read Romans 1:18-32. It tells you all people know who God is but refuse to listen and obey Him. So they end up glorifying self and become perverse in their thinking. This leads to their demise.

4. Hebrews 13:4, "Marriage is honorable among all, and the bed undefiled; but fornicators and adulterers God will judge." We do not need to make it our business to judge others. We can get others to read the Bible for themselves and learn why we don't do things like this. God will deal with them on how to get out of it and how to be forgiven.

5. Matthew 5:27-30, "You have heard that it was said to those of old, 'You shall not commit adultery.' But I say to you that whoever looks at a woman to lust for her has already committed adultery with her in his heart. And if you're right eye causes you to sin, pluck it out and cast it

from you; for it is more profitable for you that one of your members perish, than for your whole body to be cast into hell. And if you your right hand causes you for it is more profitable for you that one of your members perish, than for your whole body to be cast into hell." The point Jesus was making is that you need to clean up your soul. Your soul or heart is comprised of your mind, thoughts, feelings and being. The soul can either breathe in the breath of God or it can breathe in evil. It can lead you into doing acts of adultery. When Jesus mentioned the right eye, he was talking about the eye of the soul, which leads you to good or evil. If it leads you to do well, your body avoids going to hell. But if it leads to do evil, you may put yourself in hell and you may not be able to return from hell. You are the one who does it. To avoid this you need to ask the Lord forgiveness daily. So you don't go further into sin. To understand forgiveness by the Lord, we turn to Psalms 103:12, which states: "As far as from the east is from the west, so far has He (God) removed our transgressions from us." We are not only forgiven, but we are made so as not to remember them anymore.

In conclusion, we need to know that definition of marriage in God's word. In Genesis 2:24, it says between a man and woman. We also need to respect our mates and others by not lusting for other mates. We can do this by cleaning out the eye of our soul. We do this by confessing sin. We guard the eye of the soul from temptation such as going on line looking at dating services, porn, x-rated movies, and reading playboy or other porn books or magazines. We ask the Lord God to help us in these areas if we have trouble. When we find we are faced with a problem, we praise God and bring his presence in to help us in time of need. Remember God loves you and he wants you to do the right thing. Jesus said to the woman, who was caught in adultery, you are forgiven. Don't do it again. He says the same thing to us.

Chapter 9

Bless God and Others with Giving

The eighth positive commandment is blessing God and others through your giving. Why should you give? After all, you need the money. God knows you need to live. In fact, God owns 100% of everything. In Matthew 6:31-33, it states: "Therefore do not worry, saying 'What shall we eat?' or 'What shall we drink?' or 'What shall we wear?' For after all these things the Gentiles seek. For your heavenly Father knows that you need all these things. But seek first the kingdom of God and His righteousness and all these things shall be added to you."

In the Old Testament you were to give only a 10th of what you got to the Lord. This was set up by Abraham who we are the adopted seed. In Hebrews 7:1-3, it states: "For this Melchizedek, the king of Salem, priest of the Most High God, who met Abraham returning from the slaughter of kings and blessed him; to whom also Abraham gave a tenth part of all, first being translated "king of righteousness,' and then also king of Salem, meaning 'king of peace,' without father, without mother, without genealogy, having neither beginning of days nor end of life, but made like the Son of God, remains a priest continually." This gives us a good example of what our father Abraham did. We need to try to do the same thing. If we cannot tithe, then we need to work towards that goal. The reason to work towards it is so we can be blessed by God and also be a blessing to others. God doesn't ask for it nor does he need it. God wants you to tithe to the church out of obedience to Him.

In Luke 21:1-4, it states: "Then He looked up and saw the rich putting their gifts into the treasury, and He saw also a certain poor widow putting into two mites. So He said, 'Truly, I say to you that this poor widow has put in more than all; for all these out of their abundance have put in offerings for God, but she out of her poverty has put in all the livelihood that she had." The widow took a leap of faith knowing that someone who has God would provide for her. She was looking for heavenly rewards not earthly rewards. Now the Pharisees were giving to show how great they were and looking for rewards of men.

How can I be like the widow in our giving? Consider the following:

1. Give without show. Matthew 6:1-4 says, "'Take heed that you do not do your charitable deeds before men, to be seen by them. Otherwise you have no reward from

your Father in heaven. Therefore, when you do a charitable deed, do not sound a trumpet before you as the hypocrites do in the synagogues and in the streets, that they may have glory from men. Assuredly, I say to you, they have their reward. But when you do a charitable deed, do not let your left hand know what your right hand is doing, that your charitable deed may be in secret; and your Father who sees in secret will Himself reward you openly.'" Don't make a public speckle of yourself. Do it quietly by not drawing attention to yourself. God will reward you if you do it secretly.

2. Give according to your ability. 1Corinathians 16:1-2 says, "Now concerning the collections for the saints, as I have given orders to the churches of Galatia, so you must do also; on the first day of the week let each one of you lay something aside, storing up as he may prosper, that there are no collections when I come." Here Paul was instituting a way of giving according to their ability to give; he wanted them to set aside what they could each week. On the first day of the week, they would collect it and save it. In that way, Paul could receive it and use it to help others. It helped the Gentiles to learn to give to God. It did not put a heavy burden of the tithe on them because they were not taught to do this. He was

showing them how to build to a tithe. If you have the desire, try to give something so as to start small. That is, try giving what you can. Then increase it. God will bless you for whatever you give.

3. Be willing to give to God. 1 Chronicles 29:3-9 says, "'Moreover, because I [David] have set my affection on the house of my God, I have given to the house of my God, over and above all that I have prepared for the holy house, my own special treasure of gold and silver: three thousand talents of gold, of the gold of Ophir, and seven thousand talents of refined silver, to overlay the walls of the houses; the gold for things of gold and the silver for the things of silver, and for all kinds of work to be done by the hands of craftsmen. Who then is willing to consecrate himself this day to the Lord?' Then the leaders of the fathers' houses, leaders of the tribes of Israel, the captains of thousands and of hundreds, with the officers over the king's work, offered willingly. They gave for the work of the house of God five thousand talents and ten thousand darics of gold, ten thousand talents of silver, eighteen thousand talents of bronze, and one hundred thousand talents of iron. And whoever had precious stones gave them to the treasury of the house of the Lord, into the hand of Jehiel the Gershonite. Then the people rejoiced, for they had

offered willingly, because with a loyal heart they had offered willingly to the Lord; and King David also rejoiced greatly." As you can see, the one who gave first was the leader. When David gave, others followed his example. Notice that the whole country and its people gave. There was joy in the land. If you are willing to give it sets an example to others. You are a true leader.

4. Be ready to give. 2 Corinthians 9:5 states, "Therefore I thought it necessary to exhort the brethren to go to you ahead of time, and prepare your bountiful gift beforehand, which you had previously promised, that it may be ready as a matter of generosity and not as grudging obligation." Make sure you budget your gifts ahead of time and set aside what you want to give. In the Old Testament, a tenth of what you earned or grew was what you were to set aside for the Lord. Many people gave it first. If you cannot tithe, try to give something and work towards that goal. In a little while you will find it easier to give.

5. Be ready to follow the principles of giving. 2 Corinthians 9:6-7 reads, "But this I say: He who sows sparingly will also reap sparingly, and he who sows bountifully will also reap bountifully. So let each one give as he purposes in his heart, not grudgingly or of necessity; for God loves a cheerful giver." The widow gave because

she wanted to give not because she had to do it. She knew the Lord would provide for her. She wanted to help others. When you empty out your vessel then God can fill your vessel; God can fill up it to the top. That is the way with giving. You give what you can and God will add to it.

6. The promise of giving. 2 Corinthians 9:8 says, "And God is able to make all grace abound toward you, that you, always having all sufficiency in all things, have an abundance for every good work." God supplies all of our needs when we give back. He doesn't horrid money or things. Such things will perish in time. When we give, we are investing in the kingdom of God where treasures are eternal. We don't have to worry about where we live or what to eat. For the Lord will provide those things. We will have money in His bank account. His bank account will never go bankrupt.

7. Give proportionately. Malachi 3:10 says, "'Bring all the tithes into the storehouse, that there may be food in My house, and prove Me now in this,' says the Lord of hosts. 'If I will not open for you the windows of heaven and pour out for you such blessing that there will not be room enough to receive it.'" In this verse, we need to tithe or at least work towards tithing. By tithing we can see God will open the windows and provide for us. We

don't need to horrid money or try stealing from others and God. God will not withhold anything from His children.

In conclusion, we need to give to others and to God, so the Lord can give back to us. We also need to trust God that He is a good Daddy and will supply all of our needs. We don't need to steal from others to become rich and famous on this earth. Mathew 6:19-21 says, "'Do not lay up for yourselves treasures on earth where moth and rust destroy and where thieves break in and steal; but lay up for yourselves treasures in heaven, where neither moth nor rust destroys and where thieves do not break in and steal. For where your treasure is, there your heart will be also.'"

Chapter 10

Build Others Up with Your Words

The ninth positive commandment is building up others with your words. You should try to think the best of people. In Philippians 4:8 we find, "Finally, brethren, whatever things are true, whatever things are noble, whatever things are just, whatever things are pure, whatever things are lovely, whatever things are of a good report, if there is any virtue and if there is anything praiseworthy—meditate on these things." If we are mediating on good things we will speak of good things.

So many times a person kills another person's spirit with gossip. Gossip looks at all of the negatives of that person and diminishes him or her as a nonviable person in our society. Each person has a set task in this world to make it a better place. When we tell others negative things about them we destroy the God given talents they have or diminish them to the point that they cannot do the job God created them to do. Leviticus 19:16 says, "You shall not go about as a talebearer among your people; nor shall you take a stand against the life of your neighbor; I am the Lord."

How can we build others up? Consider the following:

1. Hear God's voice and listen to what He says to you. Consider 1 Kings 19:11-13, which states, "Then He said, 'Go out, and stand on the mountain before the Lord.' And behold, the Lord passed by, and a great and strong wind tore into the mountains and broke the rocks into pieces before the Lord, but the Lord was not in the wind; and after the wind an earthquake, but the Lord was not in the earthquake; and after the earthquake a fire, but the Lord was not in the fire; and after the fire a still small voice. So it was, when Elijah heard it, that he wrapped his face in his mantle and went out and stood in the entrance of the cave. And suddenly a voice came to him, and said, 'What are you doing here, Elijah?'" The Lord will ask you questions about what you are doing. This is how He corrects us when we do such things as bearing false witness against our brother or when we are negative towards others. Consider Psalm 95:7-8, which states, "For He is our God, and we are sheep of His pasture, and the sheep of His hand. Today, if you will hear His voice: 'do not harden your hearts, as in the rebellion, and as in the day of trial in the wilderness.'"

This same verse is found in Hebrews 3:7, and in Hebrews 15:4-7. Therefore, it must be important. We need to listen to God so we can do the right thing.

2. Ask God to help your words to be good. Psalm 19:14 says, "Let the words of my mouth and the meditation of my heart be acceptable in Your sight, O Lord, my strength and my redeemer."

3. Ask God to change your heart and mind. Psalm 51:10 states, "Create in me a clean heart, O God, and renew a steadfast spirit within me." He can help you do this by reading the word of God, that is, the Bible.

4. Look at the good in others. Proverbs 11:27 says, "He who diligently seeks good finds favor, but trouble will come to him who seeks evil." In the story of Pollyanna, Pollyanna mentions that her missionary minister father told this proverb: "If you look for the good in others you will find it, but if you look for the bad in others it will find you." Pollyanna teaches the people of her town to play the glad game and help them find the good in others. We also need to play the play the glad game, help one another to find the good in others and build them up with positive words.

5. Encourage others. In John 14:1-4 we find, "'Let not your heart be troubled; you believe in God, believe in also in Me. In my Father's house are many mansions; if it were

not so I would have told you. I go to prepare a place for you. And if I go and prepare a place for you, I will come again and receive you to Myself; that where I am there you may be also. And where I go you know, and the way you know.'"Jesus is dispelling all fear and terror of his leaving. Jesus is telling his disciples that He has a place for you in his kingdom. He is preparing that place. I have had the personal experience of an open heaven, where I saw the place where I would be in heaven. I saw a beautiful Tudor house with a garden in the back. I saw French doors that were in the back of house in front of the garden. Inside was a conservatory with realms of music on bookshelves, a white golden piano and an oboe on the piano. I also saw a beautiful white birdcage with a parakeet inside. On the cage was engraved the word Jackie. It was my pet in the cage. Just below her was Tina Marie, my tabby cat. As I went outside of the French doors, a path lead to a beautiful white stable and inside was a palomino horse, whose name was Lightning. All of my life I wanted a horse like the one I saw. I never had one. I was so filled with joy seeing it. Even though I may never have one here on this earth, I know God will have this horse waiting for me in heaven. God showed me I could come to this place anytime I wanted. I could see my family and friends who had passed away. This gave me hope to continue on the course God had set before me. I could now help to encourage others not to be down and out. God would have great things for them to see. Everyone needs to experience an open heaven and bring the Good News of Jesus Christ to others. We do this by loving them and accepting them for who they are. In this way, we can lead them to the Lord.

6. Loving kindness. Proverbs 31:26 says, "She [the wise woman] opens her mouth with wisdom, and on her tongue is the law of kindness." This shows me the perfect wise woman which I see as the Holy Spirit. The Holy Spirit has all the characteristics of a perfect mom. When I was a child, and the ministers and teachers would talk about the trinity, I could see who our Father was, and the Son where He was, and the Mother. Since there was no mention of mom I just felt in my being that the Holy Spirit was mom. In the Bible it mentions in Genesis 1:2, "The earth was without form, and void; and darkness was on the face of the deep. And the Spirit of God was hovering over the face of the waters." This verse reminds me of mom hovering over her child. It shows that she cares what happens to the earth. Just like the Holy Spirit was caring for the earth before creation was complete, we need to show loving

kindness and care to others. We also need to ask the Holy Spirit to help open our mouths with wisdom and our tongues with the law of kindness. Another example that the Holy Spirit helps with loving kindness is through teaching. 1 Corinthians 2:10-13 states: "But God has revealed them to us though His Spirit. For the Spirit searches all things, yes, the deep things of God. For what man knows the things of a man except the spirit of the man which is in him? Even so no one knows the things of God except the Spirit of God. Now we have received, not the spirit of the world, but the Spirit who is from God, that we might know the things that have been freely given to us by God. These thing we also speak, not in words that man's wisdom teaches but which the Holy Spirit teaches, comparing spiritual things with spiritual." The Holy Spirit teaches things that God wants us to know. As you see the Spirit as a teacher; our natural mothers are the primary teacher to us. It is the Holy Spirit that teaches us to be kind and gentle to others, because the Holy Spirit is kind and gentle to us.

In conclusion, we need to learn to listen to God's voice through the Holy Spirit. We need to ask Him to change our hearts and renew our spirit within us. If we have a new heart and new spirit, the Holy Spirit will help us with the words that come out of our mouths. We will be able to see the good in others. They will see the good in us. We can start encouraging others to do same thing. We can show our loving kindness to the whole world.

Chapter 11

You are Jones, the King's Kid

The tenth commandment is "I am Jones." That is, you are the King's Kid. Our God supplies all of our needs. When you see yourself in this light and you know who you are in your relationship to God, you do not need all the material goods out there; you don't need to envy others and covet their possessions. When your focus is not on God, you focus on the worldly system of me, myself and I. Instead, focus on the Trinity; that is, on God—Father, Son and Holy Spirit.

You are probably wondering how you get there. Many people are told that they must compete to get top grades. They may think they must be left brain thinkers and work in areas of math and science. They think that they must go to an Ivy League University or that they will be a no-body. On TV they are told they need all of this stuff to be somebody or they will wind up being a no-body. You can see that following all of these sayings leaves you further in the hole financially or a feeling of dissatisfaction with yourself.

First, you must stop listening to the world and start listening to God and what He has to say on the subject. Look at the teachings of Jesus and what He has to say. An example of this is in the temptation of Jesus. Matthew 4:1-11 says, "Then Jesus was led up by the Spirit into the wilderness to be tempted by the devil. And when He had fasted forty days and forty nights, afterward He was hungry. Now when the tempter came to Him, he said, 'If You are the Son of God, command that these stones become bread.' But He answered and said, 'It is written, "Man shall not live by bread alone, but by every word that proceeds from the mouth of God."'

"Then the devil took Him up into the holy city, set Him on the pinnacle of the temple, and said to Him, 'If You are the Son of God, throw Yourself down. For it was written: "He shall give His angels charge concerning you," and, "In their hands they shall bear you up, lest you dash your foot against a stone."' Jesus said to him, 'It is written again, "You shall not tempt the Lord your God."'

"Again, the devil took Him up on an exceedingly high mountain, and showed Him all the kingdoms of the world and their glory. And he said to him, 'All these things I will give You if You will fall down and worship me.' Then Jesus said to him, 'Away with you Satan! For it is written, "You shall worship the

Lord your God, and Him only you shall serve."' Then the devil left Him, and behold, angels came and ministered to Him."

This story gives you an example of what the world will do to tempt you to listen to it. What you must do is to know God's word and be prepared to answer the world back. You need to know it well enough so that the world will not misquote it to you and deceive you into going down the wrong path. You need to quote scripture back to the world of what God says about the temptation. That is, what Jesus did and you need to do the same thing.

Second, clean up your act. Listen to God about cleaning up your act. Matthew 4:17 reads, "From that time Jesus began to preach and to say, 'Repent, for the kingdom of heaven is at hand.'" You are probably asking yourself what does it mean to repent and why do I need to do so? Repent means to make a 180 degree turn in your life and head in the right direction. You need to start hearing from God. God is holy and only people who have started to clean up their acts can have a meaningful relationship with him.

Now you are wondering what and where is the kingdom of heaven? The kingdom of heaven is the place where you can meet and have a relationship with God. It is really inside of you. God will reveal in that place his plan and purpose for your life.

God will guide you every step of the way to your purpose and giftedness, and how to use them.

In Matthew 7:7-8 we find, "Ask, and it will be given to you; seek, and you will find; knock, and it will be opened to you. For everyone who asks receives, and he who seeks finds, and to him who knocks it will be opened." These are the things you do when you journal with God. You ask a question He gives you and you write down the thoughts He gives you. God can give you dreams and visions that will help you see where you are and where you will be going. If you don't understand, ask God to explain them to you in detail. He will only give you good things. He is not here to hurt you but to help you. If you have bad thoughts, disregard them, for they are from the enemy. God is positive. Satan is negative.

In my case, at age 7, God revealed Himself to me. I had experienced some life threatening illnesses. At age 7 I could not learn or do anything. The world said I was mentally retarded and would never be of much use. That is a lie. But God revealed Himself to me as a small young girl with a plaid dress, blond hair and patent leather shoes. She looked into my eyes. I heard with a loud clear voice that I would never suffer such illnesses in my life again. The strange thing was I was temporarily deaf at the time. I could not hear. The measles had left me temporarily deaf. From that day on God communicated with me. Fifty-seven years later God has helped me become a writer, illustrator, teacher, artist and musician. I am all of these things today. I give God all the honor and glory for helping me.

You too can have this relationship. He will take you from the lowest spot and lift you up. The one thing you need to remember is God is the one doing it. Not you. Don't ever let your pride get in the way and lead you to think you can do it on your own. You can't. You will need God's guidance every day of your life. Things you don't understand God will clarify for you in His word, sometimes in others and in the small audible voice. Keep on knocking, keep seeking and Keep asking God. He will be there for you. Remember, God makes you the King's Kid, or Jones if you prefer.

Chapter 12

Conclusions

How can we apply these ten positive commandments? The first thing we need to do is to worship God. We need to build the church up and teach its members to respect God. We can do this through praise and worship. We need to realize that God is God, there is no other. We need to teach our family and friends about God. We can also answer the call to be God's people. We do this by respecting God and listening to what He says.

Second, we need to honor God. How can we do this? When we wake-up in the morning we need to read his word, pray, and thank God for what he has done. We need to write down what he says to us and do what he wants us to do. We also need to meet with others and share our dreams, our visions and our writings to confirm what God is saying to us. If the dreams are positive they are from God. If they are negative they are usually from the enemy—Satan.

Third, we need to praise God. We need to learn to praise God instead of cursing God. We can start doing this by waking up in the morning and say praises to the Lord. At times we say I don't feel like praising God. That is the exactly the time we need to praise God. It brings His presence to us. The more we say the words, "Praise God," the more it brings an orchestra of praise. Praise tells us who God is, which ushers in His presence, which changes everything. It changed King David's life. It will change your life and help you see things in a more positive light. Try it and see how much better your life becomes.

As you praise God, you will see the need to keep the Sabbath holy. What does that mean? First, our body needs a day of rest from working. Just like God rested from creation work. We need to rest our bodies from work. Second, we need to feed our spirit man by reading the word of God. This helps build a positive outlook on life. Third, it is through dreams and visions that we hear from God. When you rest, God can usually speak to you. He can give you direction in your life. You need to write down what God tells you through such dreams, visions, and thoughts. If you have trouble sleeping, picture yourself with Jesus near the Sea of Galilee. Ask Jesus some questions. This way you will be able to dream and vision your journey with the Lord. Fourth is too fast. You can do a water-fast for a few days or you can fast from certain foods or things for an extended period of time. Remember to do it the proper way, not for show to the lord it over others.   The best fast is from negativity. Do positive things to others. This fast is found in Isaiah 58. This fast leads us to pray for others and it takes away the statement, "Poor me." The Lord can show you in the spirit realm what curses or negative things you can break over people and animals.

Finally, we can keep the Sabbath holy by assembling together for worship and through the sharing of ideas concerning what God has done through the week. We need to encourage each other in the faith. It gives us a chance to know what we are to do in the upcoming week. It gives us our marching orders.

As we keep the Sabbath Day holy, it brings us healing relationships with others. One of first relationships that need to heal is with our parents. We need to honor our fathers and mothers that their days may be long upon the land that the Lord gives us. It is the first commandment with a promise.

Why should you honor them when they were not there for you or they were too strict with you? Regardless of how our parents treated us, they are still our parents. You need to forgive them and honor them. Parents make mistakes. We need to see fathers as the perfect Father God and mothers as the perfect mother as experienced in the Holy Spirit. We need to tell them that that they are loved. Things will get better. Stop holding grudges over past mistakes they made. By doing this you will live long upon the land which God has given you.

As we honor our parents the next step is killing others with kindness. Jesus said in Matthew 5:43-48, "You have heard that it was said, 'You shall love your neighbor and hate your enemy.' But I say to you, love your enemies, bless those who curse you, do good to those who hate you, and pray for those who spitefully use you and persecute you, that you may be sons of your Father in heaven; for He makes His sun rise on the evil and on the good, and sends rain on the just and on the unjust. For if you love those who love you, what reward have you? Do not even the tax collectors do the same? And if you greet your brethren only, what do you do more than others? Do not even the tax collectors do so? Therefore you shall be perfect, just as your Father in heaven is perfect."

Jesus is teaching us how to bring our enemies into the kingdom by showing them loving kindness. We also need to pray. This is how we can change our negative attitudes about them. We also need to help them heal of their hurts and wounds. They are not the real enemy. They are victims of Satan. They need our help; not condemnation and judgment. We have all fallen short and missed the mark. Now is the time to forgive them and help them out. Keep making friends out of your enemies that we all can live in the kingdom of peace. This is done through kindness, love and forgiveness.

In addition to showing kindness to our enemies and loving them, we also need to respect our spouses and others. When we marry someone we take marriage vows that state we will remain with that person through better or worse, in sickness and in health, until death do us part. Another part of the wedding vows is if there is anyone knows why they should not be wed, speak now or forever hold your peace. It also mentions that no man shall put us asunder. This means no person can come between their marriages and try to destroy it.

We need to take our vows seriously. We will not always live happily ever after. There will be problems that arise. You need to work through these problems together. Together you can do anything. If you include Jesus you have a three-strand rope, and it can never be broken. In my case, when Gary took ill, I picked him up. I took his place as the bread winner until he was able to do it again. He did the same for me when I was in a car accident. He did some of the housework and made sure the house was cared for. That is what you do in a marriage relationship. You support each other.

If you have been in a failed marriage situation or divorce, learn from your mistakes. Try not to make the same mistake over again. If you do marry again try to make it work. Invite

Jesus to be the third strand in your marriage. Learn to work together.

In addition to working together with your mates, give to God and others. Here are some points 1. Give without showing. Don't make yourself great to others eyes by what you give. Do it in secret. 2. Give according to ability. This means give what you can. Learn to budget. 3. Give willingly to others. Don't have anyone use emotional blackmail to get you to give. This is not of God. Do what God tells you in your spirit; not what man says. 4. Be prepared to give. Make sure the gift is prepared ahead of time. 5. Consider the principle of giving. If you give willingly you will reap willingly, but if you have a bad attitude towards giving or begrudge God your gift, you will get nothing. 6. The promise of giving to God will supplement all of your needs. God cares for you.

Besides giving you also need to build others up. Before we can build others up we need to build up ourselves. We can do this by hearing God's voice. Listen and write down what God says about you. It will change your life. As your heart and mind are changed, you need to be in God's word to keep it changed. As you change, ask God to help you change the way you express yourself through your words. Your tongue can build people up or tear them down. What you need to do is to look for the good in people and it will find you. As you look for the good in them, they will look for the good in you. Finding good in others helps to build them up. My relationship with my mom was not always a good one. My mom saw herself in me and did not want me to fall in the same traps she fell in. Once I realized what she was doing I forgave her. I also started looking for the good in her. I was able to tell her in what ways she was like the Holy Spirit. It brought tears to her eyes. My mom has been doing better. People need to hear that they are valued individuals.

Last of all, we need to realize we are the King's Kid or as my dad would say, "Jones." When you realize that you are a child of the King, you don't need to covet other people's stuff. You have all you need. You will stop listening to the enemy. He will tell you that you need to be famous. Now you can tell him you are the King's Kid and are already famous. Satan will try to tempt you by saying, "Did God really say that?" You can say "Yes, He did say I am the King's Kid and what more do I need." Jesus did this to Satan and Satan left. Put Satan where he belongs, in hell. Claim the land back that Adam gave away. It is up to you how you are going to live your life. You can choose life and the ten positive commandments, or death and follow the law which leads to condemnation and unforgiveness. Today I choose life. Follow the ten positive commandments and the road to forgiveness.

The Ten Positive Commandments Study Guide

This study guide is to help you see a more excellent way in which God wanted to relate to his people. God wanted to meet his people on Mount Sinai to show his love and compassion. But when they rejected him, God gave the Law instead. In Jeremiah 31: 31-34, "'Behold, the days are coming, says the Lord, when I will make a new covenant with the house of Israel and with the house of Judah—not according to the covenant that I made with their fathers in the day I took them by the hand to bring them out of the land of Egypt. My covenant, which they broke, though I was a husband to them, says the Lord.

"'But this is the covenant I will make with the house of Israel after those days, says the Lord: I will put My law in their minds, and write it on their hearts; and I will be their God and they shall be My people.

"'No more shall every man teach his neighbor, and every man his brother, saying, "Know the Lord," for they all shall know Me, from the least of them to the greatest of them, says the Lord. For I will forgive their iniquity, and their sin I will remember no more.'" This is what God wanted to do in the first place.

It will help you get on the path that God wanted to do with his people Israel. Read the chapter and answer the questions for homework. In small groups, discuss the situation. In the Large Group, share your ideas.

Chapter One

Introduction

In Exodus 17 it says that after a three month journey, the Israelites are found setting camp in front of Mount Sinai, where God wants to make a covenant with them. The covenant offers many benefits, but also obligates them to obey God. The people agree to meet with the Lord. Moses prepares for the day they will meet God.

What happens on that day?

_____

_____

_____

_____

_____

Why did the people rebel against God when they said they would obey him?

_____

_____

_____

_____

_____

Would we do the same thing that the Israelites did? Why or why not?

_____

_____

_____

_____

Who can make us obey the law and how can the law be written in our hearts and minds?

_____

_____

_____

_____

In your small group discuss how we can be God's people according to Jeremiah 31:31-34.

In the large group discuss the conclusions you came up with on how we can be God's people.

Closing prayer: Lord, let your Holy Spirit rule and reign in our hearts. Write your laws in our hearts and minds. Let us be your people in everything we do and say. In Jesus' name, amen.

Chapter Two

Worship God Only

The first positive commandment is to worship God and Him alone. How do you feel you should do this commandment?

_____

_____

_____

_____

_____

What does God say about Himself?

_____

_____

_____

_____

_____

What are the things that God does for us that makes Him worthy for our praise and worship?

_____

_____

_____

_____

_____

In your small group, discuss reasons why we need to worship God.

In the large group, discuss the conclusion you came up with.

Closing prayer: Lord, we worship and praise you for all you have done. Please be with us daily and guide us down the right path. Thank you for all you have done. In Jesus' name, amen.

Chapter 3

Honor God

The second commandment is Honor God. This means God comes first in your life. What does this mean to you?

_____

_____

_____

_____

_____

To me it means when you wake up in the morning, you read your Bible. To take your journal out and listen to what God has to say to you. You have a written dialogue with God. How do you think you can do this?

_____

_____

_____

_____

Ben Franklin one time asked, "Why should I Honor God? How do I know He even exists?" What was his answer? Do you agree with him?

_____

_____

_____

_____

_____

In small groups discuss how we can Honor God.

In the large group, go over the conclusions you have reached.

Closing prayer: Lord, help us to honor you every single day of our life. We cannot do it on our own. Send your Holy Spirit to guide us in ways that honor you. In Jesus' name, amen.

Chapter 4

Praise God

The third commandment deals with praising God instead of swearing and taking the Lord's name in vain. How do we take the Lord's name in vain and what does it do to us?

_____

_____

_____

_____

_____

How can we change our behavior? How do we praise the Lord?

_____

_____

_____

_____

_____

What are some of the benefits of praising the Lord? Can it change our lives? State how it can change lives.

_____

_____

_____

_____

_____

In your small group, list the benefits of praising the Lord and how it can change lives.

In the large group, share the conclusions you have come up with.

Closing prayer: Lord, help us not to take your name in vain. Help us to praise you in all situations. Guide us in the right path in this area. Thank you for being our God and saving us from ourselves. In Jesus' name, amen.

Chapter 5

Hear God's Voice and Enter His Rest

The fourth commandment is hearing God's voice and entering His rest. What does this mean to you?

_____

_____

_____

_____

To hear God's voice, we need to be quiet. We need to pick a day, time and place to physically rest from our labors. Where in the Bible does it say to keep the Sabbath day holy? What does it mean?

_____

_____

_____

_____

_____

_____

_____

_____

_____

_____

Name some ways you can achieve this Sabbath Day rest.

_____

_____

_____

_____

_____

_____

_____

_____

_____

_____

_____

_____

In your small group, list the ways you can achieve the Sabbath Day rest.

In the large group, discuss the ways you listed to achieve the Sabbath Day rest and how can they be implemented in your life.

Closing Prayer: Lord, help us to enter your rest. Show us the time and place you want to meet with us. Help us to remain faithful to you. In Jesus' name, amen.

Chapter 6

Honor Your Father and Mother

The fifth positive commandment is to honor your father and mother. Why should we honor our parents?

_____

_____

_____

_____

_____

Your earthly father helps you relate to your heavenly Father. How is your relationship with your earthly father? Does it affect how you relate to your heavenly Father? Why?

_____

_____

_____

_____

_____

_____

_____

_____

Your earthly mother helps you relate to your heavenly Mother. Who is your heavenly Mother? How is your relationship with your earthly mother? Does it affect how you relate to your heavenly Mother? Why?

_____

_____

_____

_____

_____

_____

_____

Name six reasons why honoring our parents is important.

_____

_____

_____

_____

_____

_____

In your small group, discuss the reasons why we should honor our parents. Also, discuss your relationship with your earthly parents and any bearing on our relationship with our heavenly parent.

In your large group, discuss the results you came up with.

Closing Prayer: Lord, help us to honor our parents. So that we can have a better relationship with you. Keep us from dishonoring them. Show us a more excellent way we can honor them if we don't always agree with their philosophy. In Jesus' name, amen.

Chapter 7

Kill Others with Kindness

The sixth commandment is to kill others with kindness. Why kill anyone with kindness?

_____

_____

_____

_____

_____

Where does murder come from?

_____

_____

_____

_____

_____

How do we kill someone with kindness?

_____

_____

_____

_____

_____

How do we get rid of evil that will lead to murder?

_____

_____

_____

_____

_____

How can I be perfect like God and really forgive my enemies?

_____

_____

_____

_____

_____

In your small group, list the ways how you can get rid of evil that would lead to the murder of someone. List the ways you can kill your enemies with kindness.

In the large group, discuss your findings on how to get rid of evil that would lead you to murder and discuss the ways you can kill someone with kindness.

Closing prayer: Lord, help us to forgive our enemies. Help us to think of ways we can kill our enemies with kindness and make them our friends. In Jesus' name, amen.

Chapter 9

Bless God and Others with Giving

The eighth positive commandment is blessing others through your giving. Why should I give to others? After all, I need the money.

_____

_____

_____

_____

_____

In the Old Testament we told to tithe to God. Why should we tithe to God? He doesn't need it.

_____

_____

_____

_____

_____

In Luke 21:1-4, Jesus is looking at all the different people giving their offerings. He sees a widow that has given all she has. He mentions to his disciples that what makes her different from others is she gave out of her need. How can we be like the widow in our giving?

_____

_____

_____

_____

_____

In your small group, list the ways how you can give like the widow.

In the large group, write down the conclusions you came up with and explain to the group if this is a possible way of giving.

Closing Prayer: Lord, help us to be like the widow in our giving. Help us also not to expect to use our giving as a bribe so that we can get more out of it. Help us to be satisfied with what we have and to have great joy when we give to others to help them out in their needs.

Chapter 10

Build Others Up with Your Words

The ninth positive commandment is building up others with your words. You should think the best of people which is stated in Philippians 4:8. Then why do people gossip about others? Give me your reasons.

_____

_____

_____

_____

_____

What does gossip do to other people? How does it hurt others?

_____

_____

_____

_____

_____

_____

_____

How can we build others up?

_____

_____

_____

_____

_____

In your small group, list the ways you can build each other up.

In the large group, discuss these ways and how we can be more positive to others.

Closing Prayer: Lord, we have failed you at times with our gossip and negative ways. Help us to be more positive and try to find the good in others instead of the bad. In Jesus' name, amen.

Chapter 11

You are Jones, the King's Kid

The tenth commandment is I am Jones. I am the King's Kid. My Father God supplies all of my needs. Is this how you see yourself? Why?

_____

_____

_____

_____

_____

When you see yourself in this light, and you know who you are in your relationship with God, you do not need all of the material goods, you don't need to envy others and covet their possessions. Your focus is not on the trinity world system of me, myself and I, but rather on the Holy Trinity of God the Father, Son and Holy Spirit. You are wondering how do I get there. Ask God to show you a way you can get there. List ways you can below.

_____

_____

_____

_____

_____

_____

_____

_____

_____

_____

In your small group, make a list of ideas of what the Lord showed you.

In the large group, share your ideas.

Closing prayer: Lord, help us to be the King's Kid. Help us to worship you alone, not the God of me, myself and I. Help us to realize our true identity. Lead us on the path of being a true servant of God. Thank you for making us the King's Kid. In Jesus' name, amen.

Chapter 12

Conclusion

Now I would like you to list the ten positive commandments and tell how you can apply them to your everyday life.

1._____

_____

_____

_____

_____

_____

2._____

_____

_____

_____

_____

_____

_____

3._____

_____

_____

_____

_____

_____

4._____

_____

_____

_____

_____

_____

5._____

_____

_____

_____

_____

_____

6._____

_____

_____

7. _____

8. _____

9. _____

_____

_____

10._____

_____

_____

_____

_____

_____

_____

In your small group, discuss how you apply each commandment.

In the large group, list the best ideas you think would be helpful to others.

Closing Prayer: Lord, help us to apply these positive commandments to our everyday lives. Help us to be a servant of all. Thank you for making us your kid. In Jesus' name, amen.

Notes